www.ingramcontent.com/pod-product-compliance
Lightning Source LLC
Chambersburg PA
CBRC092058200426
4320917B00068B/1872

Blessed and Fallen

A Guide to the Angels of Heaven and Hell

Sara M Schaller

Blessed and Fallen: A Guide to the Angels of Heaven and Hell
Copyright © 2025 by Sara M Schaller

Published by Paradisus Press

All rights reserved. First printed in the United States of America. No part of this book may be used or reproduced in any manner without written permission of the copyright owner except for the use of brief quotations. For more information, address: contact@saramschaller.com.

NO AI TRAINING: Without in any way limiting the author's [and publisher's] exclusive rights under copyright, any use of this publication to "train" generative artificial intelligence (AI) technologies to generate text is expressly prohibited. The author reserves all rights to license uses of this work for generative AI training and development of machine learning language models.

978-1-7325162-9-8

Cover design by Sara M Schaller
Interior design by Sara M Schaller
Edited by Double Vision Editorial
Artwork by @joills

First Edition: September 2025

Sara M Schaller is an author and publishing professional who lives in Colorado. She likes to write stories for all ages in the fantasy genre, and her writing usually contains elements of speculative fiction and features a large cast of characters. Her prior works include *The Genesis of Seven*, *The Revelation of Three*, and *The Testament of Thirteen*. You can visit her online at: www.saramschaller.com.

Table of Contents

Introduction 2
An Infernal Compendium
    The Levels of Hell 5
    The Rivers of Hell 6
    The Occupants of Hell 12
    Theban & Sigils 14
    Seven Deadly Sins 15
        Deadly Sin of Anger 16
        Deadly Sin of Pride 18
        Deadly Sin of Envy 20
        Deadly Sin of Gluttony 22
        Deadly Sin of Greed 24
        Deadly Sin of Lust 26
        Deadly Sin of Laze 28
    Fallen Angelic Associations 30
        Birds and Animals 31
        Colors 33
        Gemstones 34
        Numerology 35
        Poisons 36
        Qliphoth 38
        Scents 40
        Tarot 41
        Tattoos 42
        Weapons 43

The Fallen 44
    Abbadona 46
    Asmodeus 50
    Balberith 54
    Beelzebub 58
    Belphegor 62
    Haborym 66
    Kushiel 70
    Leviathan 74
    Lilith 78
    Lucifer 82
    Mammon 86
    Nehema 90
    Rofocale 94
    Satan 98

So Below 102

Introduction

There would be no fallen without the blessed.

Early on in my writing journey, I learned that if I wanted to tell the story of the angels, I could not just focus on the Blessed, no matter how much I wanted to. There was another side of the story that needed to be shared, and that was the side of the Fallen.

Much of what we know about angels revolves around the mention of a war in Heaven. But what triggered that war? And who exactly was fighting? We know that whatever happened, it caused a group of angels to be cast out of Heaven and deep into Hell. We also know that the leader of this group was Samael, the former angel who is now known as Satan, or the devil. But to me, it still did not make sense because the Bible says that God created everything in this world. Then, did He create evil, too? How would we know good without evil? All this really got me thinking that perhaps evil is necessary. Perhaps it is something that was knowingly created but given to a being who could handle it, a being like Satan who used to be the most powerful angel in Heaven, a being that was a former archangel who could recognize evil and punish it.

Introduction

Now, I will come right out and say that I am not trying to dismiss evil. I believe there is true evil in this world. That is exactly why there are angels to defend against it. Trust me, there have been times when writing about the Fallen was not easy for me, but I feel it is necessary because there cannot be one side without the other. They are so tightly intertwined that the story is not complete without both the Blessed and the Fallen. So now I try to equally acknowledge them and treat them similarly in everything I do.

With that in mind, the following pages contain all there is to know about thirteen of the most well-known fallen angels as well as Lilith, who is not an angel but an essential fallen member of Hell. While there are many more beings that occupy Satan's domain, this lineup accounts for the most common figures.

An Infernal Compendium

The Levels of Hell

Throughout history, Hell has been depicted in various ways; however, one similarity spans across all interpretations. The nature of Hell is always multilayered and tiered in levels, intentionally structured to be the opposite of Heaven. My interpretation of it also matches this imagery with nine levels of Hell, symbolic of the nine days it took the fallen angels to fall.

Levels two through seven are occupied by souls of the damned, and each level is led by a fallen angel chosen by Satan. The lowest level, level nine, is a place of despair and torment, also known as Misery. Level eight, or the Eighth Cavern, is home to the five Rivers of Hell, which sit between Misery and the other levels.

Levels two through seven are each assigned a deadly sin:
- Level Two: Pride
- Level Three: Envy
- Level Four: Gluttony
- Level Five: Greed
- Level Six: Lust
- Level Seven: Laze

Elysium, the first level of Hell, is home to the devil and his brethren of fallen angels. Satan rules this level as king, and he does not allow any damned souls who succumbed to anger to reside here, as their sins cannot compare to his. Instead, these souls must remain in the ninth level of Hell, Misery, forced to be tormented for eternity.

The Rivers of Hell

There are five rivers that flow through the Eighth Cavern of Hell:
- The River of Pain
- The River of Lamentation
- The River of Forgetfulness
- The River of Fire
- The River of Hate

The rivers flow in the shape of a pentagram, and they can structure solid forms in the water, such as streams, waves, or figures, that can rise out of the riverbed. Most of the time, they remain still and instead tempt unsuspecting beings into their watery depths by luring them with words they want or need to hear, eventually soothing their victims into complacency and pulling them under. Once someone is trapped in their current, it is nearly impossible to get free, the victim forever consumed by the torments of the river. They also act as a deterrent for any damned soul who tries to escape Misery and enter the other levels of Hell, as the rivers are never successfully traversed.

The River of Pain

When caught in the River of Pain, the victim experiences constant suffering and severe discomfort, the body wracked with agony that they wish for the absence of feeling.

The River of Lamentation

When caught in the River of Lamentation, the victim experiences endless wailing and cries of grief, sounds so hopeless that they eventually join in too.

The River of Forgetfulness

When caught in the River of Forgetfulness, the victim experiences confusion and slowly loses their memory, eventually forgetting who they are and where they are, caught in a state of unknowing.

The River of Fire

When caught in the River of Fire, the victim experiences intense heat, their body continually haunted by a burning sensation.

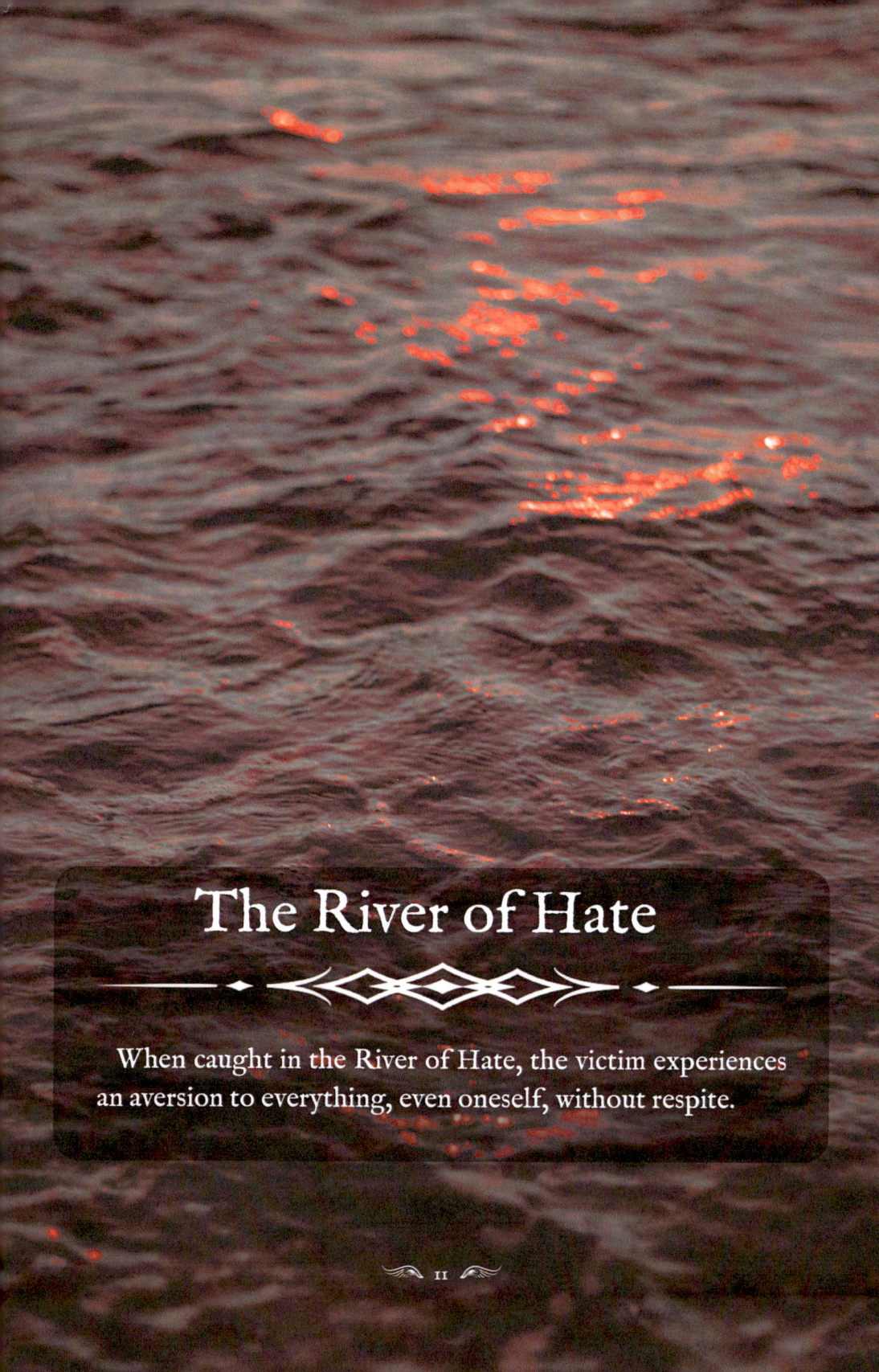

The River of Hate

When caught in the River of Hate, the victim experiences an aversion to everything, even oneself, without respite.

The Occupants of Hell

While Hell is home to the devil, there are other beings that occupy the infernal realm with him. Fallen angels are the most familiar, but there are also demons, damned souls, hellhounds, and hellcats.

Fallen Angels

Fallen angels are Satan's closest accomplices. They rebelled in Heaven and fell to Hell with him. Trust is impossible to form among the Fallen, and while Satan might not confide in them fully, he does rely on them to help bring order to the chaos.

Demons

Demons are creatures that like to torment the damned souls and enjoy causing chaos in Hell. No one knows where they come from or how they originated, but it is believed there is a separate demon region that they were exiled from. The demons in Hell are considered lesser demons since they are incapable of possession. Satan tolerates them, but finds them to be annoying.

Damned Souls

Damned souls are human spirits condemned to Hell after death for their sins and wrongdoings. They are the majority in Hell; however, they could never overthrow the Fallen, as they are intangible and lack the strength. Their presence in Hell irritates Satan immensely. He would prefer they all go to Purgatory.

Hellhounds

Hellhounds are common in Hell and act as guards between the levels to avoid damned souls from wandering. Each hellhound is trained by Leviathan to cooperate, learn commands, and follow Satan's orders. They enjoy hunting and tormenting damned souls, and particularly like to eat them, although Leviathan tries to restrain them from doing so.

Hellcats

Hellcats are less common in Hell, and no sighting has been reported for centuries. They are not easy to train and are not cooperative. Instead, they prefer their independence and privacy. The Fallen refuse to call them extinct because the sounds of meowing are occasionally heard echoing in the caves.

Theban & Sigils

Theban is the written language of the fallen angels. Today, it is associated with magic and considered the "Witches' Alphabet." Throughout the book, you will see each fallen angel's name written in Theban. The chart below is a preview of the alphabet.

A	B	C	D	E	F	G	H	I	J	K	L	M

N	O	P	Q	R	S	T	U	V	W	X	Y	Z

a	b	c	d	e	f	g	h	i	j	k	l	m

n	o	p	q	r	s	t	u	v	w	x	y	z

Additionally, each member of the Fallen has a sigil, or circular crest, that they use to identify themselves, which will also be included in every profile.

Seven Deadly Sins

The deadly sins are linked to emotions that are intense, raw, and excessive. Fallen angels embrace these emotions, letting them drive their actions and decisions. For them, sin is freedom, the characteristic that sets them apart from the Blessed. Conversely, in Heaven, emotion is moderated; it is not something that is freely expressed. Because of this, the Fallen believe that blessed angels do not have free will. Sin also goes against divine order, which stands as an act of continuing rebellion against God, a fact that immensely entertains the Fallen. Now let's explore the seven deadly sins in detail.

Anger	Red
Pride	Purple
Envy	Green
Gluttony	Orange
Greed	Yellow
Lust	Pink
Laze	Blue

Deadly Sin of Anger

Anger is a strong feeling of hostility. It leads to rage, violence, bloodshed, and brutality when unchecked. Oftentimes, anger is expressed physically through fighting and movement. For the Fallen, anger is a positive trait, viewed as a sign of power and authority. The heavenly virtue opposite anger is patience.

Deadly Sin of Pride

Pride is a strong feeling of arrogance. It leads to narcissism, condescension, snobbery, and pompousness when unchecked. Oftentimes, pride is expressed verbally, mentally, and physically through words, thoughts, and body language. The heavenly virtue opposite pride is humility.

Deadly Sin of Envy

Envy is a strong feeling of jealousy. It leads to covetousness, resentment, discontent, and bitterness when unchecked. Oftentimes, envy is expressed verbally and mentally through words and thoughts of longing for someone else's possessions or qualities. The heavenly virtue opposite envy is charity.

Deadly Sin of Gluttony

Gluttony is a strong feeling of overindulgence. It leads to excess, immoderation, decadence, and dissatisfaction when unchecked. Oftentimes, gluttony is expressed physically through excessive eating or drinking. The heavenly virtue opposite gluttony is temperance.

Deadly Sin of Greed

Greed is a strong feeling of selfishness. It leads to materialism, possessiveness, yearning, and abundance when unchecked. Oftentimes, greed is expressed mentally or physically through the want of wealth and the many acts one will pursue to gain it. The heavenly virtue opposite greed is kindness.

Deadly Sin of Lust

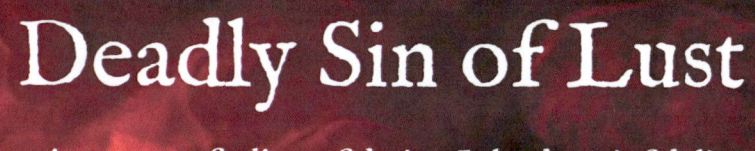

Lust is a strong feeling of desire. It leads to infidelity, deceit, betrayal, and debauchery when unchecked. Oftentimes, lust is expressed physically and mentally through sensual acts or thoughts. The heavenly virtue opposite lust is chastity.

Deadly Sin of Laze

Laze, more commonly known as sloth, is a strong feeling of laziness. It leads to carelessness, ignorance, negligence, and indolence when unchecked. Oftentimes, laze is expressed physically, or rather as a lack of physical expression, due to avoidance of activity. The heavenly virtue opposite laze is diligence.

An Infernal Compendium

Fallen Angelic Associations

The fallen angels are connected to ten topics. Some of them match the Blessed associations, but there are a few that are unlike their counterparts or are interpreted differently. This is mainly because the Fallen do not want to be like the Blessed, even though they once were one in the same. Not every fallen angel will be connected to every association, mainly because they are limited in number. Specific connections will be noted in each fallen angel's profile.

Birds and Animals

Fallen angels still maintain their strong connection to birds, one of the only associations that remain intact after their rebellion and fall. Each bird and fallen angel are paired based on the personality traits they share; however, their correlation is beyond symbolic. It is physical, too. The fallen angel can call the bird and speak to it or can have them carry paper messages. If needed, the fallen angel can even see through the bird's eyes in the sky.

Bird	Traits
Condor	Insight, clarity, strength
Cormorant	Persistence, stubborness, confidence
Hummingbird	Independence, adventurousness, passion
Kestrel	Clarity, power, agility
Kingfisher	Adventurousness, impulsivity, abundance
Parrot	Boisterousness, talkativeness, sociability
Pelican	Practicality, resourcefulness, cooperation
Pigeon	Loyalty, adaptability, resilience
Raven	Vigilance, observation, fearlessness
Rooster	Alertness, protectiveness, fertility
Shoebill	Quiet, patience, observation
Stygian Owl	Darkness, mystery, wisdom
Swan	Balance, grace, loyalty
Woodpecker	Persistence, determination, self-reliance

An Infernal Compendium

Spirit animals—or animal totems—on the other hand are only paired for symbolic significance. Each fallen angel likes to choose an animal they feel embodies their personality and then uses it as heraldry, even fashioning rings that look like the animal and wearing it daily. Typically, their choice of animal becomes a part of their identity in Hell.

Bat	Intuition, fearlessness, flexibility
Bear	Strength, protectiveness, agility
Bull	Determination, productivity, fertility
Cougar	Speed, stealth, assertiveness
Dog	Loyalty, protectiveness, cooperation
Ferret	Cunning, stealth, intelligence
Frog	Intuition, flexibility, inconsistence
Goat	Hardiness, stubbornness, fearlessness
Monkey	Curiosity, agility, intelligence
Otter	Adaptability, rebelliousness, independence
Pig	Honesty, indulgence, uncleanliness
Racoon	Cleverness, cunning, resourcefulness
Snake	Intensity, passion, assertiveness
Turtle	Adaptability, longevity, patience

An Infernal Compendium

Colors

While color can be linked to energy, the Fallen prefer to focus on how color conveys emotion and influences mood. Certain shades evoke feelings that can affect how someone is perceived or judged when it comes to the occupants of Hell. Not only is each fallen angel linked to a certain color but the deadly sins themselves are connected to colors as well, given how intertwined the sins are as a display of excessive emotion.

Black	Power and authority
Blue	Loyalty and reliability
Coral	Boldness and optimism
Green	Envy and judgment
Ice Blue	Tranquility and clarity
Magenta	Assertiveness and respect
Orange	Energy and sociability
Pink	Sensitivity and playfulness
Purple	Ambition and irritability
Red	Aggression and strength
Scarlet	Passion and danger
Seafoam	Self-consciousness and charm
Silver	Reflection and dignity
Yellow	Deception and egotism

Gemstones

As the entire body is made up of energy and affected by it, gemstones are helpful tools to protect from external energetic forces, regardless of whether they are beneficial or harmful. In Hell, most of the energy is undesirable and damaging, so each fallen angel chooses a gemstone representing how it will best aid in defending against unwanted negative energy.

Amber	Purification, emotional balance, healing
Black Tourmaline	Grounding, protection, mental clarity
Cat's Eye	Prosperity, confidence, concentration
Coral	Courage, vitality, confidence
Hematite	Strength, stability, enhanced focus
Jet	Grounding, balance, purification
Malachite	Transformation, protection, self-awareness
Moonstone	New beginnings, feminine energy, inner peace
Onyx	Good luck, change, sharpened judgment
Opal	Creativity, inspiration, truth
Pearl	Resilience, personal growth, inner peace
Pyrite	Confidence, abundance, protection
Sunstone	Leadership, independence, personal power
Turquoise	Positivity, stress relief, self-expression

An Infernal Compendium

Angel's Trumpet	Affects the nervous system	Hallucination, seizure, paralysis
Death Camas	Affects the heart	Cardiac arrest, respiratory distress, coma
Foxglove	Affects the heart	Irregular heartbeat, low blood pressure, confusion
Hellebore	Affects the skin	Difficulty breathing, blindness, vomiting
Hemlock	Affects the digestive tract	Respiratory distress, muscle paralysis, convulsions
Jimsonweed	Affects the nervous system	Delirium, dilated pupils, bizarre behavior
Manchineel	Affects the digestive tract and skin	Blistering of mouth and throat, difficulty swallowing and breathing
Monkshood	Affects the digestive tract	Abdominal pain, confusion, chemical-smelling breath
Mountain Laurel	Affects the heart	Respiratory distress, unconsciousness, palpitations
Nightshade	Affects the digestive tract and skin	Hives, itching, bloating
Oleander	Affects the nervous system	Delirium, lethargy, blurred vision
Poison Ivy	Affects the skin	Itching, blistering, swelling
Rosary Pea	Affects the digestive tract	Organ failure, fever, lethargy
White Baneberry	Affects the heart	Cardiac arrest, respiratory paralysis, stomach cramps

Qliphoth

Qliphoth and the Tree of Death are the inverse of Kabbalah and the Tree of Life (see Blessed Angelic Associations). Qliphoth is a realm of evil and impurity that is overseen by Lilith and occupied by demons and fallen angels. The Ten Adverse Sefirot, shown below, are different attributes or branches of the Qliphoth Tree of Death (source: *The Kabbalah & Magic of Angels*, González-Wippler). A fallen angel oversees each branch, and the tree itself is full of negative energy and chaos.

Thamiel	Duality in God
Chaigidel	Confusion of the Power of God
Sathariel	Concealment of God
Gamchicoth	Devourers
Golachab	Burning Bodies
Thagirion	Those Who Bellow Grief and Tears
Harab Serapel	Ravens of the Burning God
Samael	The Desolation of God
Gamaliel	Polluted of God
Nehemoth	Night Specters

An Infernal Compendium

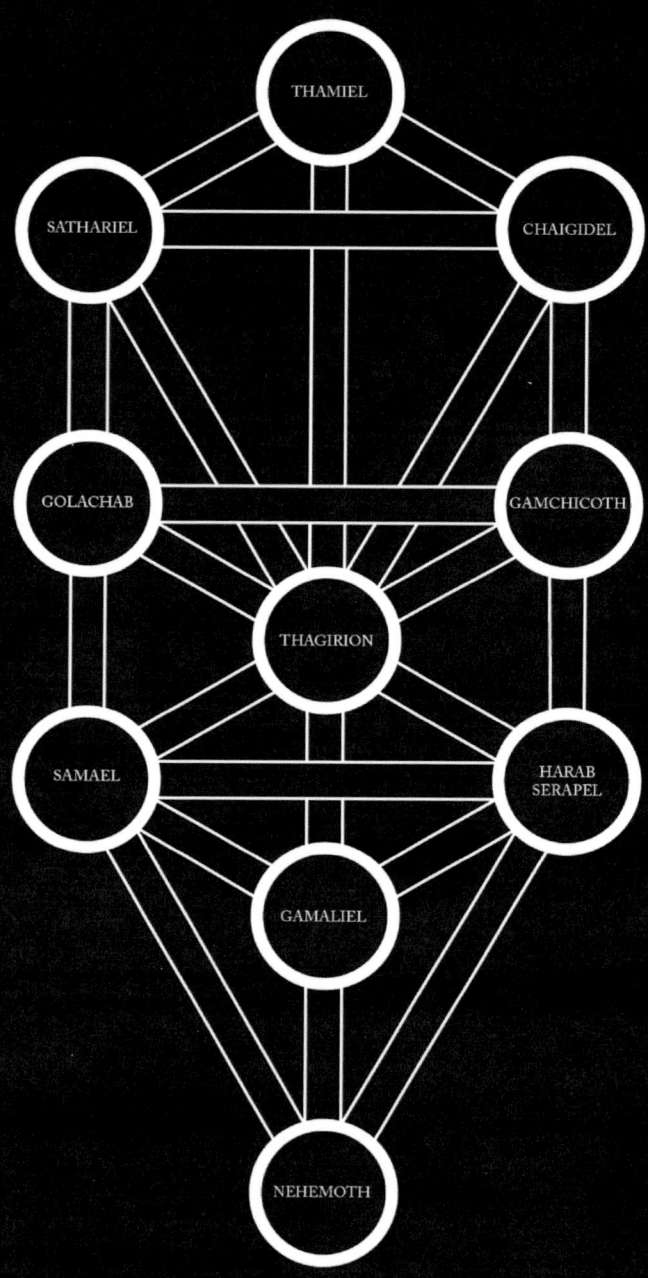

Scents

Scent conveys emotion and personality, so scent is a way to identify the fallen angels, as each carries a unique smell that closely relates to their character. For the Fallen, every association is an opportunity to display their worth or prowess. Scent not only leaves a lasting impression but can mean the difference between being categorized as strong or weak, predator or prey.

Agave	Fresh and earthy
Amaretto	Rich and warm
Bourbon	Sweet and spicy
Cigar	Woody and spicy
Citrus	Zesty and refreshing
Dark Musk	Sensual and rich
Eucalyptus	Clean and earthy
Gardenia	Floral and heady
Hemp	Pungent and earthy
Leather	Rich and warm
Teakwood	Musky and sophisticated
Tobacco	Smoky and pungent
Tuberose	Lush and sweet
Verbena	Herbal and lemony

Tarot

Tarot is a deck of seventy-eight cards that are used for divination or spiritual guidance. The deck contains the Major Arcana, which are twenty-two cards of figures, and the Minor Arcana, which are fifty-six cards divided into four suits: cups, pentacles, swords, and wands. Tarot is popular among the occupants of Hell, both played as a game, which was its original use, or used more seriously to tell fortunes. The Fallen identify with specific cards that they feel match their character.

Major Arcana	The Fool, The Magician, The High Priestess, The Empress, The Emperor, The Hierophant, The Lovers, The Chariot, Strength, The Hermit, The Wheel of Fortune, Justice, The Hanged Man, Death, Temperance, The Devil, The Tower, The Star, The Moon, The Sun, Judgment, The World
Minor Arcana	Cups, Pentacles, Swords, Wands (with Ace, Two, Three, Four, Five, Six, Seven, Eight, Nine, Ten, Page, Knight, Queen, and King of each suit)

Tattoos

Tattoos are significant to fallen angels because they are an act of freedom. While in Heaven, angels were marked with tattoos, but they were minimal and small, only present to display names or honors bestowed upon them. Conversely, the Fallen choose to ink themselves with whatever fancies them. Some tattoos are symbolic and used to convey honors. Many are just decoration that pleases the fallen angel or expresses their character. However, in Hell, the more ink one has on their skin, the more favored they are in the eyes of others.

Weapons

All fallen angels in Hell are armed with weapons. Most are stolen, either from one another or from the Forge directly. Some are crafted for a specific fallen angel, a luxury mainly given to Satan and those he deems valuable like the leaders he appoints in each level. Whether in Heaven or Hell, a weapon is considered more powerful when it is engraved with the name of the bearer. The Fallen engrave their names in Theban on the handle of their weapons. They also decorate the objects with their chosen gemstone to imbue the tool with their protective qualities.

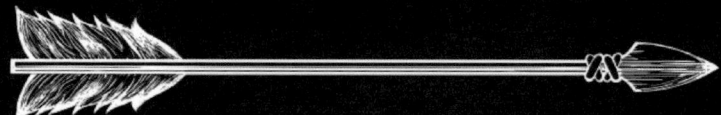

Abbadona

Abbadona (ABBA-DONNA) is a fallen angel who keeps to herself. She resides in the eighth level of Hell, home to the five Rivers of Hell. These rivers try to tempt unsuspecting beings into their watery depths, but Abbadona is immune to their calls. Prior to the fall, she was a Seraphim, the highest ranked among the Blessed and, as such, very powerful.

Abbadona has extraordinary gifts that went unnoticed in Heaven, which is why she chose to side with Satan's rebellion. This fact is also why she is linked to envy; she has formidable magical power that was never appreciated, and she always wished she would be utilized as the other Seraphim were. In Hell, Abbadona is associated with the number eight because of her connection to the eighth level of Hell. The number eight is also significant to Satan since it is symbolic of his prior location, or home, in the celestial hierarchy. Now Abbadona, who resides in level eight, represents his new home, as he feels most comfortable around her. While Abbadona possesses and wields magic, she does not partake in black magic and instead practices safely within the limits. She is not evil. She is powerful and understands the need for balance.

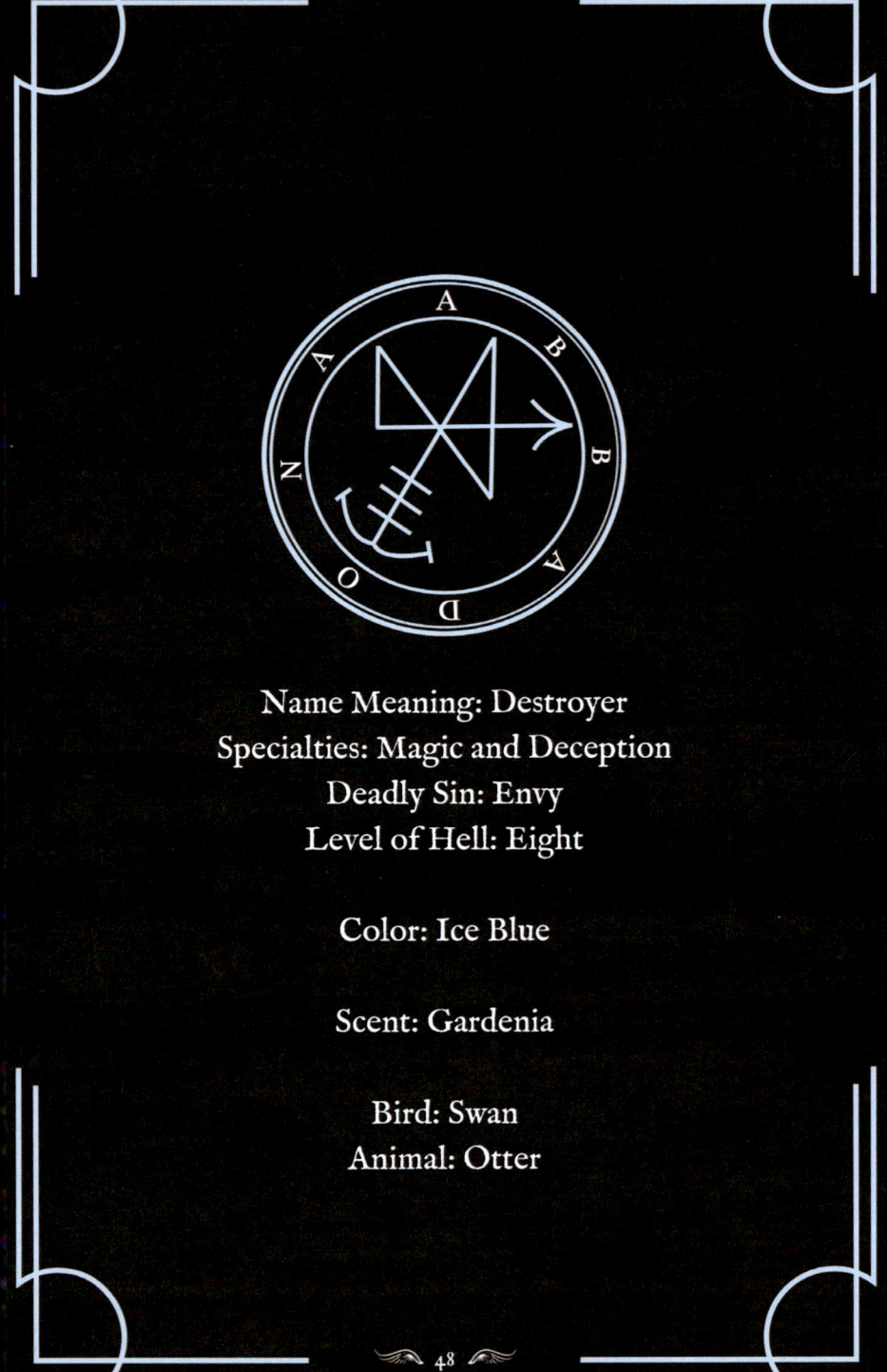

Name Meaning: Destroyer
Specialties: Magic and Deception
Deadly Sin: Envy
Level of Hell: Eight

Color: Ice Blue

Scent: Gardenia

Bird: Swan
Animal: Otter

Gemstone: Moonstone

Poison: Nightshade

Number: Eight

Tarot: The High Priestess

Tattoo(s): Moon Phases and Skull

Adverse Sefirot of the Qliphoth: Thagirion

Weapon(s) of Choice: Staff

Asmodeus

Asmodeus (AS-MO-DEE-US) is a superficial fallen angel more concerned with outward appearances than internal beauty. He is obsessed with his image and always has pristine manicured nails and gorgeous long, flowy locks. Fine designer clothes complete the look, all of it making him undeniably attractive. While Asmodeus is good at luring someone in, be it a human, demon, or fallen angel, he is also good at disappearing once he gets what he wants.

Asmodeus is associated with lust because he constantly pleasures himself either with materialistic possessions or sexual acts. He is connected to the number six because it signifies love. Asmodeus is also leader of the sixth level of Hell, which is assigned to lust and all the damned souls who succumb to it.

Prior to the fall, Asmodeus was classified as an angel of the home in Heaven. His prior duty of fostering relationships was vital to his vocation and now amplifies the sin of lust within him now.

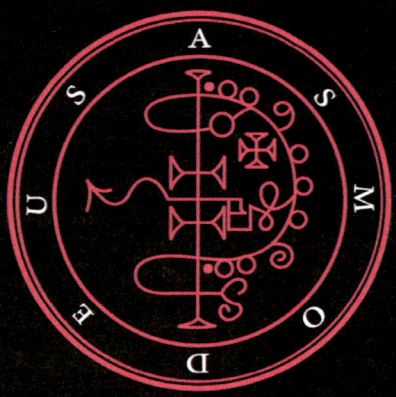

Name Meaning: Evil Spirit
Specialties: Vanity and Hedonism
Deadly Sin: Lust
Level of Hell: Six

Color: Pink

Scent: Amaretto

Bird: Rooster
Animal: Bull

Gemstone: Pearl

Poison: Foxglove

Number: Six

Tarot: The Lovers

Tattoo(s): Bull and Skull

Adverse Sefirot of the Qliphoth: Golachab

Weapon(s) of Choice: Saber

Balberith

Balberith (BALL-BURR-RITH) is a hardworking fallen angel who serves Satan in his throne room. There, Balberith attends to the spirits who have pleas by watching them, recording their requests, and then escorting them back to where they belong in Hell. When he is not working, Balberith has a gifted voice and enjoys serenading the other fallen angels during parties.

Balberith is connected to gluttony because he has a tempting voice that encourages excess. It is rumored that he travels to the human world to use his voice to inspire an overindulgence in drink. Satan assigned him the number twelve as his rank because it is symbolic of divine order, and Balberith is the only fallen angel who tries to maintain order in the chaos of Hell.

Prior to the fall, Balberith was classified as an angel of music in Heaven. He was actually among the Angels who served as guardian angels, but he failed his position by causing his human to perish. His past in entertaining others is what amplifies the sin of gluttony within him now, as Balberith never knows when to stop.

Name Meaning: Lord of the Covenant
Specialties: Impatience and Strictness
Deadly Sin: Gluttony
Level of Hell: One

Color: Seafoam

Scent: Agave

Bird: Pelican
Animal: Turtle

XII

Gemstone: Turquoise

Poison: Mountain Laurel

Number: Twelve

Tarot: The Chariot

Tattoo(s): Sea Waves

Weapon(s) of Choice: Dagger

Beelzebub

Beelzebub (BILL-ZE-BUB) is a brawny fallen angel who is appreciated by Satan for his strength and size. However, Beelzebub's keenness for excessive brawling has led to many hits on the head, resulting in forgetfulness. Unlike other fallen angels who enjoy fighting, Beelzebub does not anger easily. He is a levelheaded being who likes the adrenaline of using his strength to gain a win.

Beelzebub is associated with gluttony because of his overindulgence in fighting and betting. While he likes using his fists in a good fight, he is not strategic and often loses. The fourth level of Hell is assigned to gluttony and all the damned souls who succumb to it. Beelzebub is connected to the number four because he is the leader of this level.

Prior to the fall, Beelzebub was classified as an angel of power in Heaven. His past training as a warrior and his unwillingness to know when to yield is what amplifies the sin of gluttony in him now.

Name Meaning: Lord of the Flies
Specialties: Overindulgence and Forgetfulness
Deadly Sin: Gluttony
Level of Hell: Four

Color: Orange

Scent: Cigar

Bird: Parrot
Animal: Pig

Gemstone: Amber

Poison: White Baneberry

Number: Four

Tarot: The Fool

Tattoo(s): Pig and Skull

Adverse Sefirot of the Qliphoth: Gamchicoth

Weapon(s) of Choice: Battle Hammer

Belphegor

Belphegor (BELL-FA-GOR) is an apathetic fallen angel who seems to show no interest in anything. Taking orders does not bother him since he has no conviction to lead, but he fulfills the actions required at his own pace, which often infuriates Satan. However, when Belphegor does eventually complete a task, the result is rather ingenious, which is why Satan tolerates him.

Belphegor is the laziest fallen angel in Hell. The seventh level of Hell is assigned to laze and all the damned souls who succumb to it. It is the last level in Hell that the souls of the damned can occupy without full torment. For Satan, the fact that level seven is last means that Belphegor is last in his eyes. Belphegor is also the leader of this level, which contributes to the association.

Prior to the fall, Belphegor was classified as an angel of nature in Heaven. His past care for plants has sparked a curiosity in the cultivation of medicinal drugs, like marijuana, which amplifies the sin of laze. He always felt like he was classified wrong though because he could only keep cannabis plants alive. Everything else he killed. He actually is skilled with technology, so perhaps being an angel of art would have suited him better.

Name Meaning: Lord of the Gap
Specialties: Pessimism and Inattention
Deadly Sin: Laze
Level of Hell: Seven

Color: Blue

Scent: Hemp

Bird: Pigeon
Animal: Goat

Gemstone: Cat's Eye

Poison: Hemlock

Number: Seven

Tarot: The Hermit

Tattoo(s): Goat and Skull

Adverse Sefirot of the Qliphoth: Gamaliel

Weapon(s) of Choice: Sickle

Haborym

Haborym (HA-BORE-RIM) is the armorer of Hell. She forges all the weapons and armor for the fallen angels and personally crafts whatever Satan requests. However, Haborym keeps her truly inventive creations to herself, as she believes she is the only one deserving to possess such masterpieces. While metalworking is her true passion, she understands the intricacies of every weapon and, as such, is a lethal asset in combat.

Haborym is connected to greed because she does not like to share and hoards her finer concepts to herself. Satan assigned her the number ten as her rank because the number is symbolic of perfection, which is what Satan believes her weapons represent.

Prior to the fall, Haborym was classified as an angel of art in Heaven. Her past experience in forging weapons for the heavenly army is what amplifies the sin of greed within her now since she was never able to keep or use anything she created.

Name Meaning: Destructive Fire
Specialties: Craftsmanship and Precision
Deadly Sin: Greed
Level of Hell: Five

Color: Coral

Scent: Citrus

Bird: Kingfisher
Animal: Monkey

Gemstone: Coral

Poison: Oleander

Number: Ten

Tarot: The Magician

Tattoo(s): Oleander and Skull

Weapon(s) of Choice: Cutlass

Kushiel

Kushiel (KU-SHE-EL) is a fallen angel of punishment. He resides in the lowest level of Hell where the damned souls must complete their sentences of torment. He is stern but loves a good competition and can be quite the trickster, letting damned souls think they can win a game for their freedom when, in reality, the odds are always against them.

Kushiel is connected to envy because he is covetous of the glory that awaits in the other levels of Hell. Even though he enjoys his job, Kushiel believes he is capable, even deserving, of a higher rank. In Hell, he is connected with the number nine since he commands the ninth level of Hell.

Prior to the fall, Kushiel was classified as an angel of healing in Heaven. His past familiarity with healing now gives him the ability to hurt and inflict pain, which amplifies the sin of envy as he deals with his thoughts of lack by punishing others who are defenseless.

Name Meaning: The Rigid One
Specialties: Competitiveness and Dishonesty
Deadly Sin: Envy
Level of Hell: Nine

Color: Scarlet

Scent: Bourbon

Bird: Woodpecker
Animal: Racoon

Gemstone: Pyrite

Poison: Rosary Pea

Number: Nine

Tarot: The Tower

Tattoo(s): Skeleton Bones and Skull

Weapon(s) of Choice: Hook Swords

Leviathan

Leviathan (LUH-VAI-UH-THIN) is a fallen angel who strives for perfection. He is meticulous in everything he does, especially when it comes to Satan's commands. Leviathan is also fiercely loyal, and on the surface, that appears to be a beneficial quality but is actually a lethal threat. He will kill if directed. He trains the hellhounds to obey Satan's orders and is particularly close with Cerberus, the three-headed dog who resides in Hell.

Leviathan is associated with envy because he easily becomes jealous, especially of Lucifer, not for the qualities he possesses but of his rank. Leviathan believes he is more qualified to be Satan's second-in-command and attempts to be dutiful to display this. He is connected to the number three because his talents are overshadowed by Lucifer, who is second only to Satan himself. If Lucifer were not around, Leviathan would easily take on that role. Leviathan is also the leader of the third level of Hell, which contributes to the association. The third level is assigned to envy and all the damned souls who succumb to it.

Prior to the fall, Leviathan was classified as an angel of teaching in Heaven. His past thirst for knowledge is what amplifies the sin of envy within him now, as he desires to be an asset to Satan and feels his wisdom is the key to winning favor.

Name Meaning: Twisted
Specialties: Perfection and Loyalty
Deadly Sin: Envy
Level of Hell: Three

Color: Green

Scent: Verbena

Bird: Kestrel
Animal: Dog

Gemstone: Malachite

Poison: Monkshood

Number: Three

Tarot: The Moon

Tattoo(s): Three Headed Dog and Skull

Weapon(s) of Choice: Crescent Axe

Lilith
ՀՄՀՄԴԿ

Lilith (LIL-LITH) is the first wife of Adam, created at the same time as he was, with the intent to be equals. But that was short-lived, as Adam wanted superiority over Lilith. She refused and was punished by being turned into a snake, popularly known as the serpent in the Garden of Eden. In this form, she tempted Eve, knowing this would be the ultimate revenge to get both Eve and Adam expelled from the garden. While Lilith was a scorned victim, she is still classified as one of the Fallen because she is a trickster and her actions have always been extremely vindictive, her obsession with power driving her to commit evil acts.

While Lilith is not a being who resides in Hell, she is still closely connected to it, having spent time there and holding an immense desire to rule it. She is linked to pride because she is proud of her power, not only as a master of black magic but a temptress. She loves nothing more than manipulating others to commit an uncharacteristic act. Lilith is also connected to the number one as the first wife of Adam but, more importantly, as the first woman. She is not associated with a prior vocation since she never resided in Heaven.

Name Meaning: Belonging to the Night
Specialties: Revenge and Temptation
Deadly Sin: Pride

Color: Black

Scent: Dark Musk

Bird: Stygian Owl
Animal: Snake

Gemstone: Black Tourmaline

Poison: Manchineel

Number: One

Tarot: The Empress

Tattoo(s): Snakes

Adverse Sefirot of the Qliphoth: Chaigidel

Weapon(s) of Choice: Rondel Dagger, Bullwhip, and Metal Claws

Lucifer

Lucifer (LU-SI-FER) is a confident fallen angel who acts as Satan's second. For this reason, the two are often confused, which does not particularly bother Lucifer, as he is happy to be credited as being the king of Hell. Actually, he perpetuates the misidentification and never corrects the mistake; he prefers the glory that comes with the title. However, he knows how much it angers Satan, so Lucifer grovels respectfully to keep his rank as second-in-command, a role he originally attained by succumbing to Satan's authority, knowing his subservience would eventually grant him favor.

Lucifer is the epitome of pride. He is arrogant and gains great satisfaction from all his achievements. He is also quite sadistic, since he gains great pleasure from killing others. Lucifer is connected to the number two because of his role as Satan's second-in-command. He is also leader of the second level of Hell, which further contributes to the association. The second level is assigned to pride and all the damned souls who succumb to it.

Prior to the fall, Lucifer was classified as an angel of power in Heaven. His past willingness to help others in need is what amplifies the sin of pride within him now, as he is only consumed by thoughts of how to help himself.

Name Meaning: Bearer of Light
Specialties: Malice and Narcissism
Deadly Sin: Pride
Level of Hell: Two

Color: Purple

Scent: Teakwood

Bird: Condor
Animal: Cougar

Gemstone: Sunstone

Poison: Death Camas

Number: Two

Tarot: The Emperor

Tattoo(s): Cougar, Skull, and Sun

Adverse Sefirot of the Qliphoth: Samael

Weapon(s) of Choice: Falchion Sword

Mammon

Mammon (MAM-MON) is a truly evil fallen angel who enjoys watching others suffer. He particularly loves to strike fear in whomever he meets, either through his appearance or his actions. It is rumored that his interactions with the human world revolve around crime, mainly in the dealings of illicit drugs. It is thought that he likes getting humans hooked on an addiction because he has many and wants to inflict the same pain on others.

Mammon is associated with greed because he craves money and will not hesitate to harm others in trying to gain wealth. The fifth level of Hell is assigned to greed and all the damned souls who succumb to it. Mammon is connected to the number five because he is the leader of this level.

Prior to the fall, Mammon was a Cherubim, one rank below the top in Heaven. Even though he held a position so high, Mammon still participated in Satan's rebellion because he felt snubbed by the lack of honor he received for his rank. However, he had a hard time conforming to his role, as he always wanted more and was never happy. Mammon's past resentments are what amplifies the sin of greed in him now.

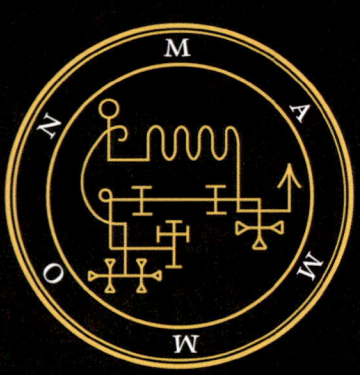

Name Meaning: Material Wealth
Specialties: Fear and Ruthlessness
Deadly Sin: Greed
Level of Hell: Five

Color: Yellow

Scent: Tobacco

Bird: Cormorant
Animal: Frog

Gemstone: Jet

Poison: Poison Ivy

Number: Five

Tarot: The World

Tattoo(s): Frogs, Poison Ivy, Creepy Clown, and Skull

Adverse Sefirot of the Qliphoth: Harab Serapel

Weapon(s) of Choice: Giant Cleaver

Nehema

Nehema (NAH-HE-MA) is an ambitious fallen angel ready to do whatever she can to benefit herself. She wishes for higher rank and wants a leadership role in one of the levels of Hell, so rumors, gossip, and secrets are her game. Nehema oftentimes offers her body in exchange for information but enjoys the pleasure and power she gains from such interactions. But one should never cross her, as Nehema is spiteful and will seek to offend or hurt others for their wrongdoings.

Nehema is connected to lust because she truly enjoys sex and is open to all partners, no matter their orientation. Satan assigned her the number eleven as her rank since she is eager to obtain a command position and eleven signifies advancement and growth.

Prior to the fall, Nehema was classified as an angel of the home in Heaven. Her past in attending to the wants and needs of others is what amplifies the sin of lust within her now. She remains a people person, with a natural gift when it comes to listening to others, but it is all for her own benefit, to twist people to her will.

Name Meaning: Pleasant
Specialties: Dominance and Spite
Deadly Sin: Lust
Level of Hell: Six

Color: Magenta

Scent: Tuberose

Bird: Hummingbird
Animal: Ferret

Gemstone: Opal

Poison: Hellebore

Number: Eleven

Tarot: The Sun

Tattoo(s): Hummingbird, Hellebore, and Skull

Adverse Sefirot of the Qliphoth: Nehemoth

Weapon(s) of Choice: Recurve Bow

Rotocale

Rofocale (ROW-FO-CAL) is the leader of the army in Hell. He is a masterful warrior and often trains other fallen angels in the art of combat and warfare. He served under Satan's command when they both were still in Heaven and now continues to support him in Hell. Rofocale is an independent fallen angel, and as such, he keeps to himself. He enjoys having a purpose and serving his king, but he does not require being showered with the glory of his achievements. He operates behind the scenes and very few know he is around. Satan likes this about Rofocale and keeps him as a secret weapon.

Rofocale is associated with anger because he is brutal in battle and causes significant bloodshed. Satan assigned him the number zero as his rank because this number is connected to nothingness and Rofocale is covert, his presence never detected. He is the only other fallen angel Satan will let claim anger as their sin as he sees many similarities between himself and Rofocale.

Prior to the fall, Rofocale was classified as an angel of power in Heaven. His past restraint in battle is what amplifies his brutality and the sin of anger in him now.

Name Meaning: The One Who Flees Light
Specialties: Stubbornness and Solitude
Deadly Sin: Anger
Level of Hell: One

Color: Silver

Scent: Eucalyptus

Bird: Shoebill
Animal: Bat

Gemstone: Hematite

Poison: Jimsonweed

Number: Zero

Tarot: The Hanged Man

Tattoo(s): Chains and Skull

Adverse Sefirot of the Qliphoth: Sathariel

Weapon(s) of Choice: Gladius

Satan

Satan (SAY-TEN), better known as the Devil and the ruler of Hell, is a bold fallen angel who fought for freedom from the divine. Satan maintains a few attributes of his former self but chooses to disassociate with his angelic past as much as possible. He prefers to be depicted as a true fallen angel instead of a monstrous creature. Satan and Lucifer are not one in the same; they are two separate beings and their names should not be used interchangeably.

Satan is full of so much wrath that it is like a fire within him. In Hell, he correlates the number one with anger, as it is his sin and he is the supreme authority. The first level of Hell is assigned to anger; however, Satan refuses to believe that any damned soul can have a temper like his, so none are allowed in his domain. Even though Satan likes the number one, he prefers to associate with thirteen. He does not want to only be defined by his sin. He feels thirteen is the number he was created with and embraces the unlucky connotations as a reminder of his rebellion.

Prior to his fall, Satan was classified as an angel of power in Heaven. His past ferocity as the most powerful warrior in Heaven is now what amplifies his reign over Hell and the sin of anger within him.

Name Meaning: Adversary
Specialties: Authority and Valor
Deadly Sin: Anger
Level of Hell: One

Color: Red

Scent: Leather

Bird: Raven
Animal: Bear

Gemstone: Onyx

Poison: Angel's Trumpet

Number: Thirteen

Tarot: The Devil

Tattoo(s): Flames, Skulls, Feathers, Bear, and King of Spades

Adverse Sefirot of the Qliphoth: Thamiel

Weapon(s) of Choice: Broadsword

So Below

As Above

Gemstone: Onyx

Zodiac Sign: Ophiuchus
Celtic Astrology Sign: Elder

Weapon(s) of Choice: Broadsword

Ancient Wonder of the World: Stonehenge
Natural Wonder of the World: Giant's Causeway
Modern Wonder of the World: The Empire State Building

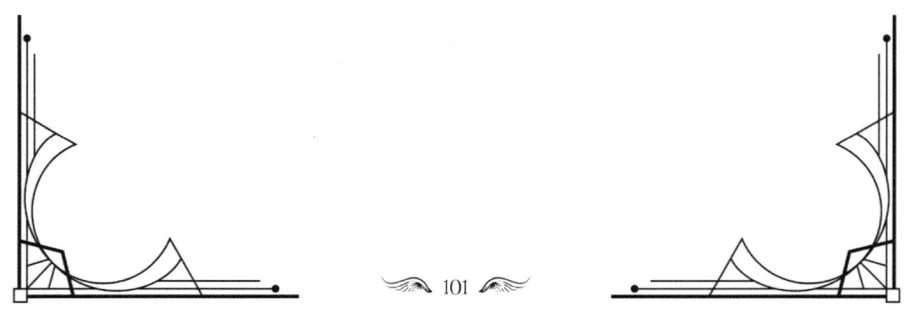

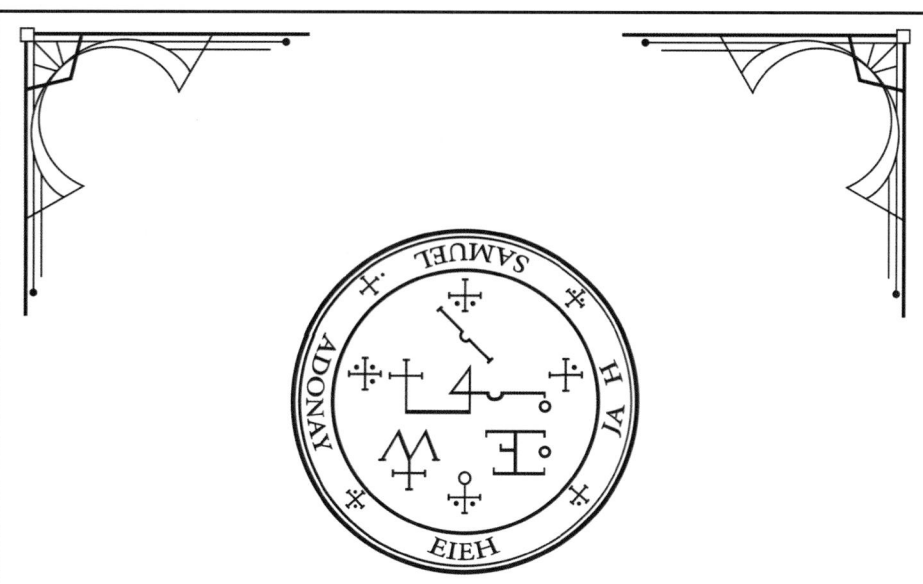

Name Meaning: Poison of God
Specialties: Strength and Truth
Circle of Vocation: Angel of Power

Color: Black

Scent: Patchouli

Bird: Raven
Animal: Bear

Archangel Samael (SAM-MY-EL), classified as an angel of power, was the favored angel—the strongest, the one most capable of handling anything God commanded. That is, until he rebelled and caused war in Heaven. Most know him now as Satan or the devil, but before his rebellion, he was just like any other angel with the same correlations and duties. Most of his associations have now been reinterpreted as symbols of evil or have completely been disregarded as relating to him. But no matter what, Samael remains within the memory of Heaven and its angelic occupants, even though attempts have been made to erase him.

Samael was fascinated with numerology, the study of number symbolism. For Samael, the numbers one, eight, and thirteen were most special. One signified supremacy, eight was his home within the celestial hierarchy, and thirteen was his ranking among the archangels. The latter is now considered an unlucky number.

Samael

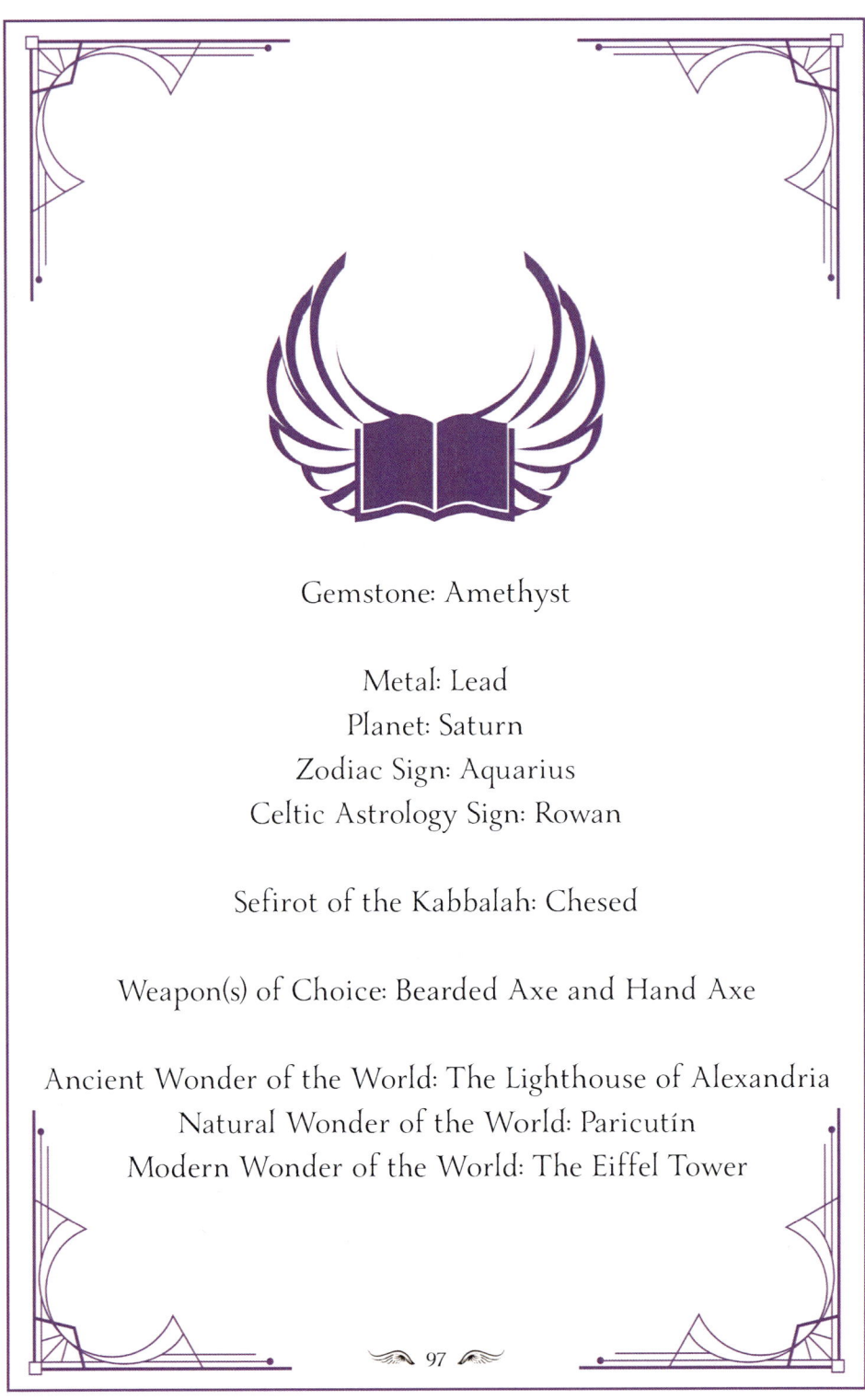

Gemstone: Amethyst

Metal: Lead
Planet: Saturn
Zodiac Sign: Aquarius
Celtic Astrology Sign: Rowan

Sefirot of the Kabbalah: Chesed

Weapon(s) of Choice: Bearded Axe and Hand Axe

Ancient Wonder of the World: The Lighthouse of Alexandria
Natural Wonder of the World: Paricutín
Modern Wonder of the World: The Eiffel Tower

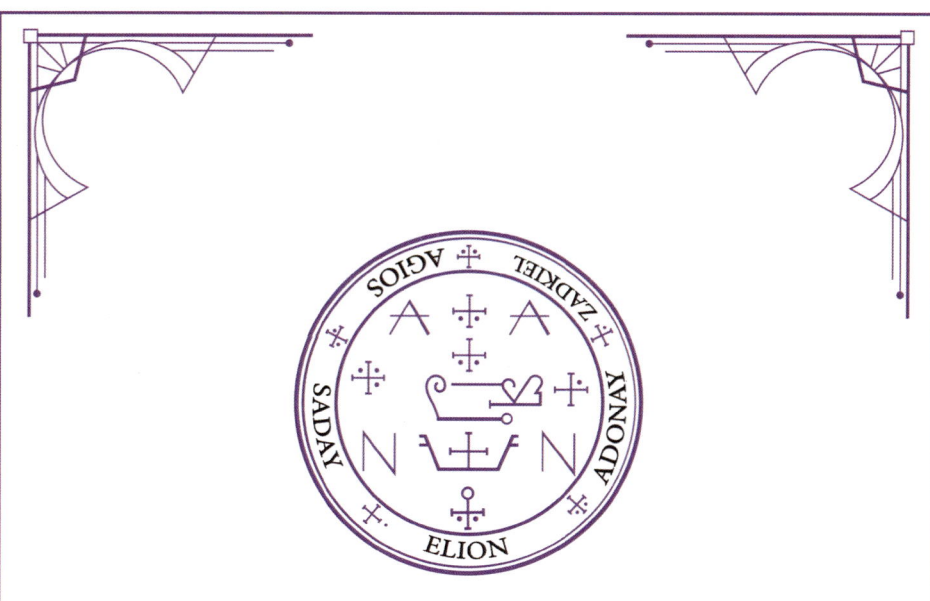

Name Meaning: Righteousness of God
Specialties: Teaching and Wisdom
Circle of Vocation: Angel of Teaching

Day of the Week: Saturday
Month: February

Color: Purple
Chakra: Third Eye

Scent: Pine

Bird: Hawk
Animal: Badger

Archangel Zadkiel (ZAHD-KEE-EL), classified as an angel of teaching, is a wise angel who loves to impart knowledge to others. He takes a humble approach to doing so, preferring the student to seek out the teacher rather than the teacher coercing the student to learn something they have no interest in. He is always reading and feels most at peace when he is surrounded by books.

Zadkiel is one of the archangels connected to the wonders of the world. One of the ancient wonders of the world is the Lighthouse of Alexandria. This structure is associated with Zadkiel since Alexandria was home not just to the Lighthouse but also the Great Library, which housed a large collection of texts from all the cultures and religions of the known world.

Zadkiel

Gemstone: Ruby

Metal: Silver
Planet: Moon
Element: Earth
Zodiac Sign: Sagittarius
Celtic Astrology Sign: Reed

Sefirot of the Kabbalah: Netzach

Weapon(s) of Choice: Long Bow and Cross Bow

Ancient Wonder of the World: The Great Pyramid of Giza
Natural Wonder of the World: Mount Everest
Modern Wonder of the World: The Great Wall of China

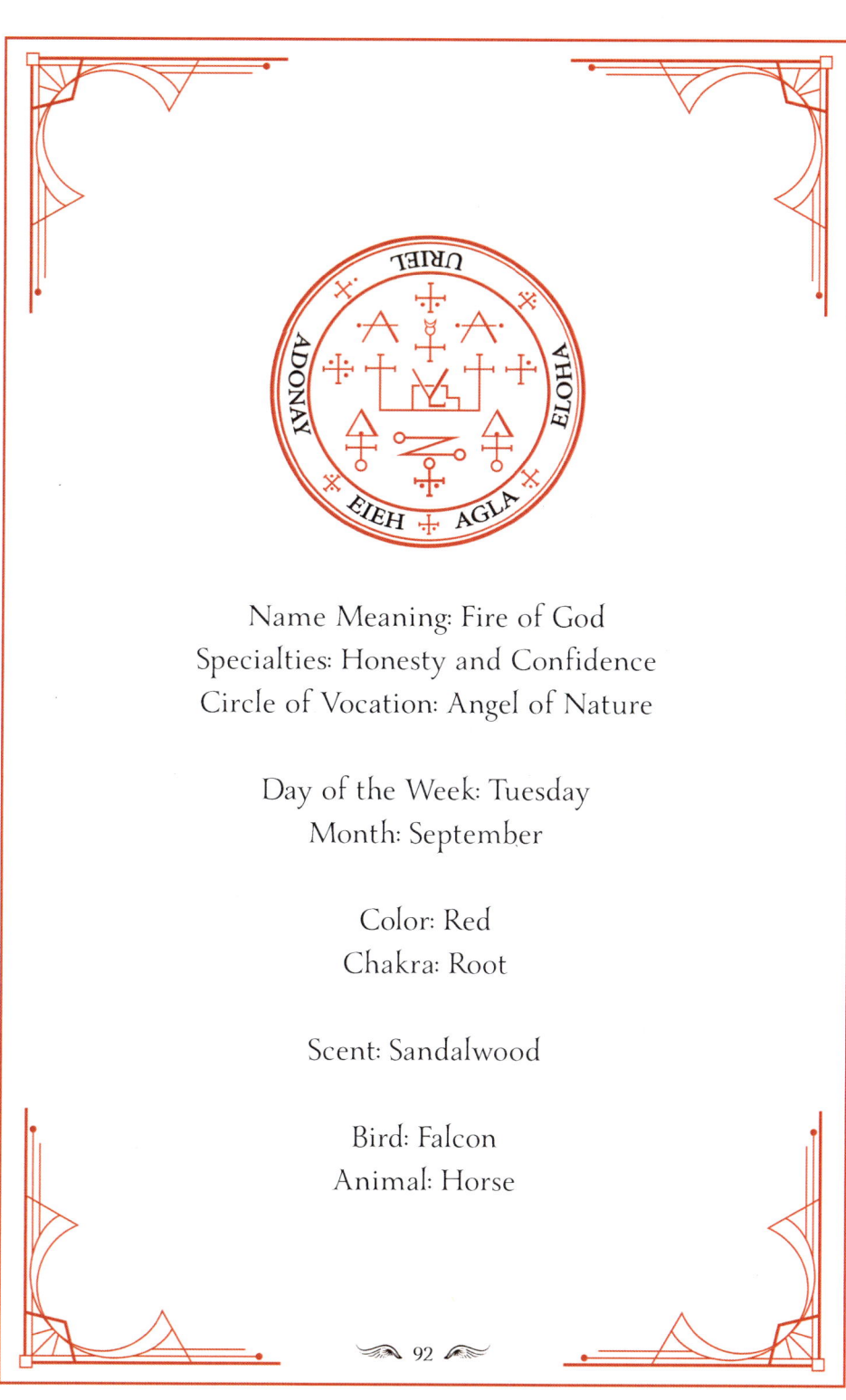

Name Meaning: Fire of God
Specialties: Honesty and Confidence
Circle of Vocation: Angel of Nature

Day of the Week: Tuesday
Month: September

Color: Red
Chakra: Root

Scent: Sandalwood

Bird: Falcon
Animal: Horse

Archangel Uriel (YOUR-EE-EL), classified as an angel of nature, is never afraid to speak his mind and make his presence known. He is most at peace outside among the trees and is associated with the outdoors. Additionally, he is believed to be the angel who chased Adam and Eve out of the Garden of Eden with the flaming sword.

Uriel is closely connected to horses, which is unusual since the animal can typically sense angelic energy and is often spooked by it. However, Uriel is like a horse whisperer; he's able to calm them.

Uriel

Bird: Puffin
Animal: Rabbit

Gemstone: Tanzanite

Metal: Copper
Planet: Venus
Zodiac Sign: Cancer
Celtic Astrology Sign: Holly

Sefirot of the Kabbalah: Hod

Name Meaning: Contemplation of God
Specialties: Love and Cherish
Circle of Vocation: Angel of the Home

Month: May

Color: Lavender

Scent: Lavender

Archangel Tzaphkiel (ZAHF-KEE-EL), classified as an angel of the home, is a friendly angel who is joyous to be around. She is a skilled seamstress who creates new apparel as well as repurposes existing garments.

Tzaphkiel's other interest besides sewing is love. Many refer to her as the angel who loves love. From familial relationships to budding romances and marriages, she enjoys seeing people committed to each other and fostering a life together. Tzaphkiel is associated with puffins, a bird that mates for life, a perfect pairing for her interests.

Tzaphkiel

Bird: Thunderbird
Animal: Bison

Gemstone: Fulgurite

Metal: Brass
Planet: Neptune
Zodiac Sign: Pisces
Celtic Astrology Sign: Ash

Sefirot of the Kabbalah: Malkuth

Name Meaning: Brother
Specialties: Dreams and Communication
Circle of Vocation: Angel of Nature

Month: July

Color: Tan

Scent: Sage

    Archangel Sandalphon (SAN-DAL-FON), classified as an angel of nature, is a quiet but mighty angel with a peaceful energy. He is incredibly wise and believed to be the prophet Elijah, who transformed into an angel on his ascent to Heaven.

    Many associate Sandalphon and Metatron as twin brothers, which explains the meaning of Sandalphon's name, which is known to be "Brother." Sandalphon interacts with the spirit world much like a shaman, a person who bridges the physical and astral planes. Sandalphon particularly likes to use dreams to communicate.

Sandalphon

Bird: Peacock
Animal: Elephant

Gemstone: Iolite

Metal: Quicksilver
Planet: Mercury
Zodiac Sign: Capricorn
Celtic Astrology Sign: Birch

Sefirot of the Kabbalah: Chokmah

Name Meaning: Secret of God
Specialties: Mysticism and Discovery
Circle of Vocation: Angel of Teaching

Month: December

Color: Turquoise

Scent: Ocean

Archangel Raziel (RAZZ-EE-EL), classified as an angel of teaching, is an inquisitive angel, known as the angel of mysteries, who likes to explore how the elements of the universe are interconnected.

Raziel enjoys writing and is the assumed author of *The Book of Raziel*, otherwise known as *The Book of Secrets*, which is divided into five sections and contains celestial and earthly knowledge. One significant topic of writing for Raziel is Jewish mysticism, like the Kabbalah, and its divine wisdom and esoteric insights.

Raziel

Gemstone: Emerald

Metal: Tin
Planet: Jupiter
Element: Water
Zodiac Sign: Scorpio
Celtic Astrology Sign: Ivy

Sefirot of the Kabbalah: Binah

Weapon(s) of Choice: Spear and Knife

Ancient Wonder of the World: The Hanging Gardens of Babylon
Natural Wonder of the World: Victoria Falls
Modern Wonder of the World: La Sagrada Familia

Name Meaning: God Has Healed
Specialties: Healing and Inspiration
Circle of Vocation: Angel of Healing

Day of the Week: Wednesday
Month: November

Color: Green
Chakra: Heart

Scent: Rose

Bird: Barn Owl
Animal: Wolf

Archangel Raphael (RAFF-EYE-EL), classified as an angel of healing, is a gentle angel who feels responsible for everyone's welfare. He wishes health and happiness to every being and hopes everyone can experience this in their life.

Raphael is an expert healer. From a simple cold to a broken bone or a major surgery, he is always there to lend a healing hand to those who need it. Raphael is cognizant of modern medical procedures as well as holistic healing. He is a strong believer in the power of herbs and gemstones just as much as medicine.

Raphael

Gemstone: Lapis Lazuli

Metal: Iron
Planet: Mars
Element: Fire
Zodiac Sign: Leo
Celtic Astrology Sign: Oak

Sefirot of the Kabbalah: Geburah

Weapon(s) of Choice: Longsword and Dagger

Ancient Wonder of the World: The Statue of Zeus at Olympia
Natural Wonder of the World: Aurora Borealis
Modern Wonder of the World: The Colosseum

Name Meaning: Who Is As God
Specialties: Bravery and Justice
Circle of Vocation: Angel of Power

Day of the Week: Monday
Month: August

Color: Blue
Chakra: Throat

Scent: Wood Smoke

Bird: Bald Eagle
Animal: Lion

Archangel Michael (MY-KELL), classified as an angel of power, is a commanding angel with a mighty presence. He is a natural leader, in charge of the Heavenly Army, and all those under his command trust him immensely. His actions are calculated, always anticipating his opponent.

Michael is the presumed judge on Judgment Day, weighing souls and determining their fates. He is often depicted in art as vanquishing the devil and dispelling evil.

Michael is a warrior, and a warrior's greatest tool is their weapon. Michael's sword contains a lapis lazuli stone in the center of the hilt, and the handle bears his name.

Bird: Dove
Animal: Lamb

Gemstone: Diamond

Metal: Gold
Planet: Sun
Zodiac Sign: Virgo
Celtic Astrology Sign: Hazel

Sefirot of the Kabbalah: Kether

Name Meaning: Angel of the Lord
Specialties: Meditation and Thought
Circle of Vocation: Angel of Teaching

Month: April

Color: White

Scent: Lily

Archangel Metatron (META-TRON), classified an angel of teaching, is a powerful angel who is often depicted as an elder due to his wise persona and the immense amount of knowledge he possesses. He is a strict rule follower and does not like to stray from the divine order of things. Metatron is closely connected to God, and many believe that he is the prophet Enoch who transformed into an angel on his ascent to Heaven.

Metatron meditates often because he is prone to having visions, which he records and then stores in Heaven. During one such vision, Metatron documented the symbol known as Metatron's Cube, shown below in his seal. It is a sacred geometry symbol, which is a shape that reflects the balance and harmony found in the universe. Sacred geometry symbols are often found in architecture, art, and nature. Metatron's Cube has become a helpful aid to focus on during meditation because it shows how energy flows through the universe.

Metatron

Bird: Crane
Animal: Tiger

Gemstone: Citrine

Zodiac Sign: Libra
Celtic Astrology Sign: Vine

Weapon(s) of Choice: Samurai Sword and Sai

Ancient Wonder of the World: The Colossus of Rhodes
Natural Wonder of the World: Harbor of Rio de Janeiro
Modern Wonder of the World: Angkor Wat

Name Meaning: Beauty of God
Specialties: Creativity and Calmness
Circle of Vocation: Angel of Art

Day of the Week: Friday
Month: October

Color: Yellow
Chakra: Solar Plexus

Scent: Jasmine

Archangel Jophiel (JOE-FEE-EL), classified as an angel of art, has a wide array of interests and expertise. Modern tools and inventions fascinate him, particularly in the field of aviation, and he likes that humans can experience flying in planes.

Jophiel is interested in the science of preserving historical artifacts. He is a skilled painter but likes to dabble with sculpture and pottery as well.

Jophiel represents balance, and for angels, the balance of energy is vital since angels are full of light and must control how much they emit, especially when interacting with humans.

Jophiel

Gemstone: Danburite

Metal: Cobalt
Planet: Pluto
Element: Air
Zodiac Sign: Gemini
Celtic Astrology Sign: Hawthorn

Sefirot of the Kabbalah: Yesod

Weapon(s) of Choice: Scythe and Sickle

Ancient Wonder of the World: The Mausoleum of Halicarnassus
Natural Wonder of the World: The Grand Canyon
Modern Wonder of the World: The Taj Mahal

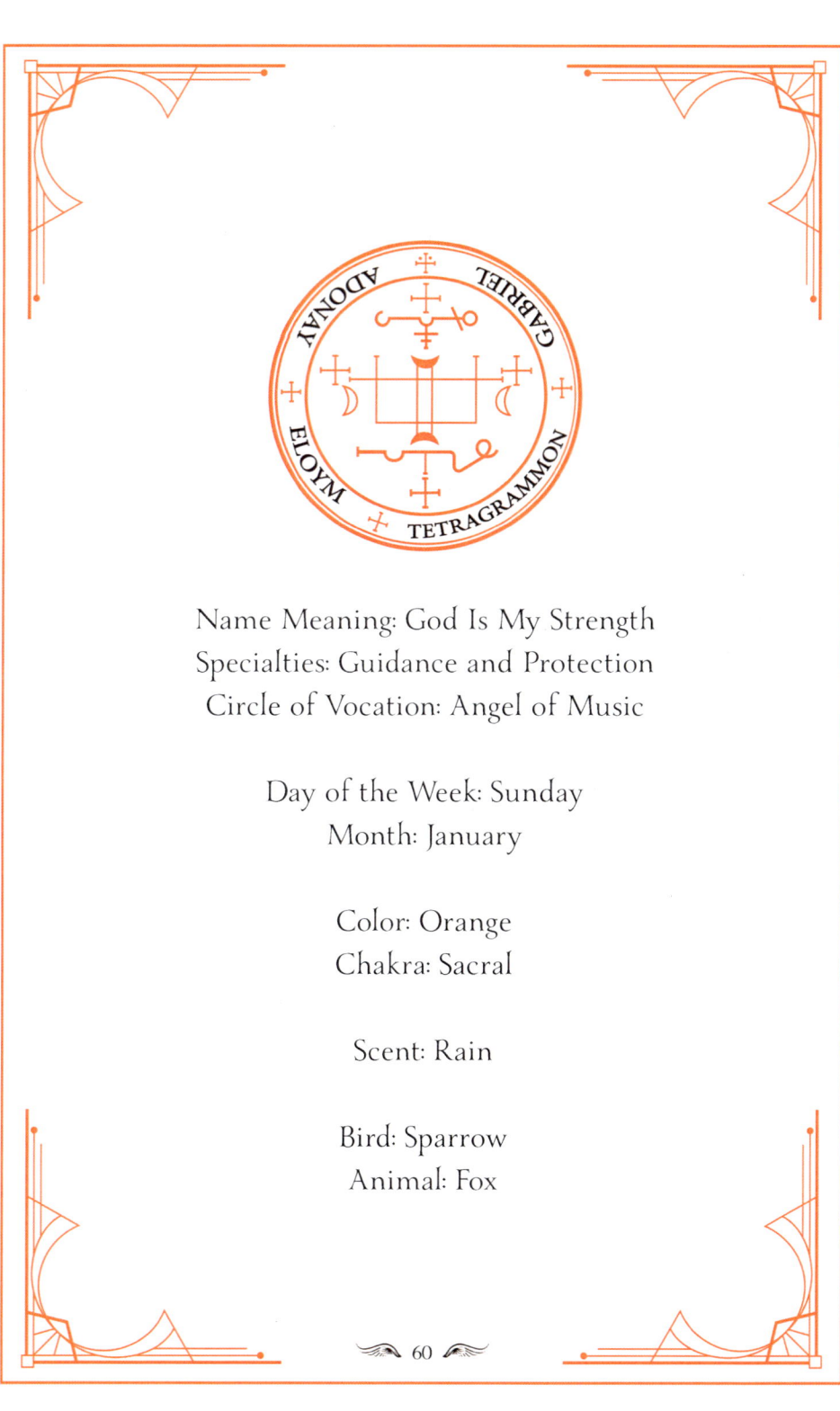

Name Meaning: God Is My Strength
Specialties: Guidance and Protection
Circle of Vocation: Angel of Music

Day of the Week: Sunday
Month: January

Color: Orange
Chakra: Sacral

Scent: Rain

Bird: Sparrow
Animal: Fox

Archangel Gabriel (GABE-REE-EL), classified as an angel of music, is a soothing and serene angel who enjoys composing melodies on his violin. It is presumed that Gabriel is the angel who blows the horn to announce the coming of Judgment Day.

Gabriel's presence makes everyone feel safe, even Mary, the mother of God, who he appeared before during the annunciation and announced that she would have a child. It is believed that all humans are touched by Gabriel before they are born, the indent on one's upper lip left behind from his finger.

In astrology, Gabriel is connected to Gemini, the star sign of the twins, because he can be depicted as a male named Gabriel or a female named Gabrielle.

Gabriel

Gemstone: Rose Quartz

Metal: Platinum
Planet: Uranus
Zodiac Sign: Taurus
Celtic Astrology Sign: Willow

Sefirot of the Kabbalah: Tiphareth

Weapon(s) of Choice: Spiked Ball Mace and Batons

Ancient Wonder of the World: The Temple of Artemis at Ephesus
Natural Wonder of the World: The Great Barrier Reef
Modern Wonder of the World: The Acropolis of Athens

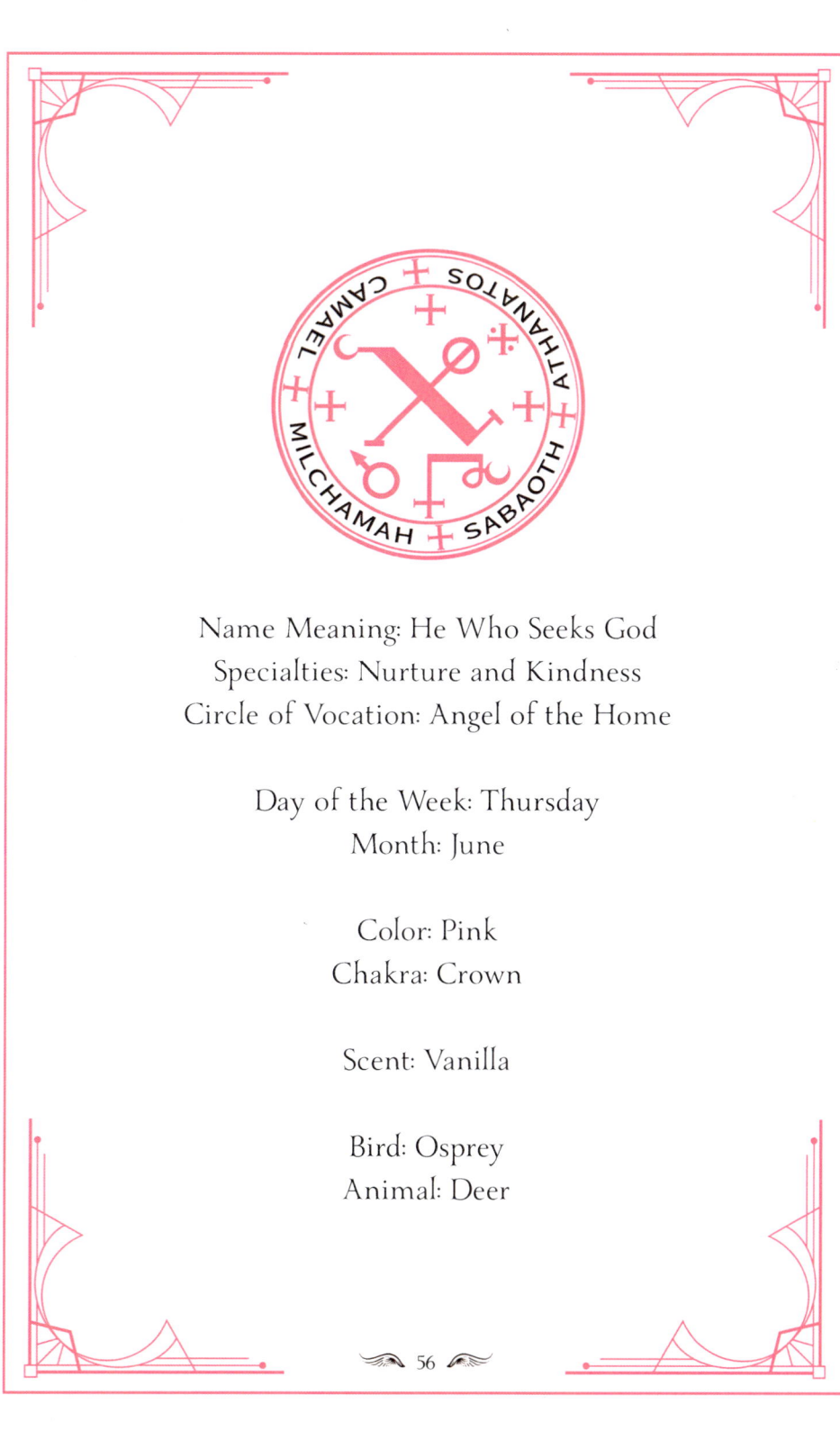

Name Meaning: He Who Seeks God
Specialties: Nurture and Kindness
Circle of Vocation: Angel of the Home

Day of the Week: Thursday
Month: June

Color: Pink
Chakra: Crown

Scent: Vanilla

Bird: Osprey
Animal: Deer

Archangel Chamuel (CHAM-U-EL), classified as an angel of the home, is a welcoming and kind angel who will immediately envelope you in a hug upon meeting him. He is the embodiment of comfort and always knows exactly what is needed to cheer you up.

Chamuel is the patron angel of chefs and bakers, and prefers sweet desserts to savory dishes, not for the taste—angels cannot partake in food—but for the culinary preparation. Since Chamuel is unable to taste food, he relies on scent to craft dishes. Herbs and spices are staples, but his favorite smell is that of vanilla, not only because it is a key ingredient in baking but because it is sweet and comforting, two words he would use to describe himself.

Bird: Harpy Eagle
Animal: Jackal

Gemstone: Yellow Calcite

Weapon(s) of Choice: Claymore Sword

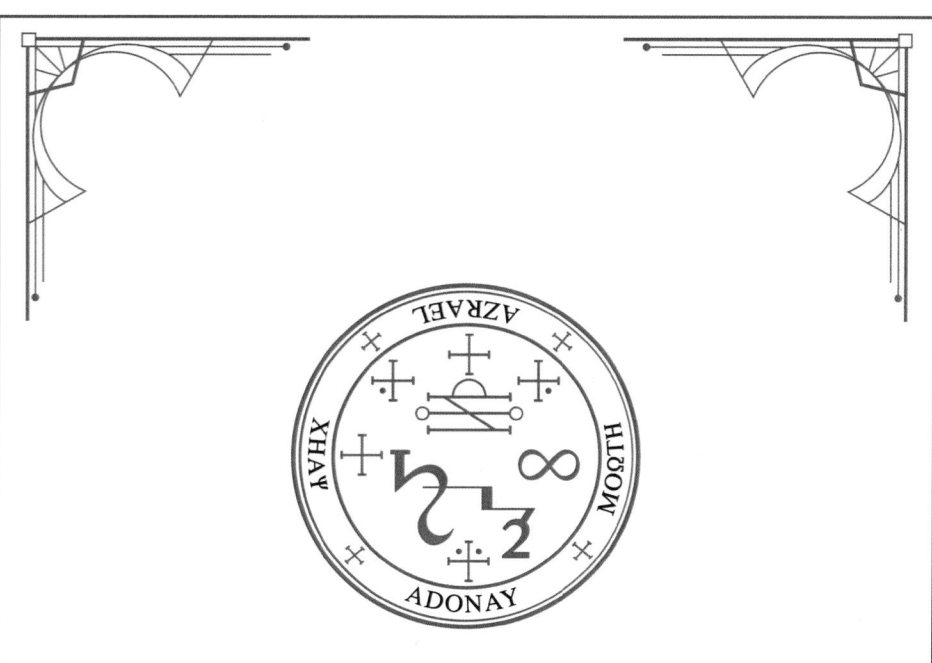

Name Meaning: Whom God Helps
Specialties: Transition and Comfort
Circle of Vocation: Angel of Healing

Color: Gray

Scent: Frankincense

Archangel Azrael (AS-RAY-EL), classified as an angel of healing, is otherwise known as the Angel of Death, an elusive angel, perhaps since death is not something to seek. Although Azrael is commonly associated with death, he is also there to act as a comforting presence during times of transition and the grieving process.

Azrael is sometimes depicted as the grim reaper, but he is not an angel to fear, as he grants miracles of life, too. Azrael understands the intricacies of life and death, and as such, he is associated with alchemy and the daunting search for everlasting life.

Azrael

Bird: Cardinal
Animal: Ram

Gemstone: Bloodstone

Zodiac Sign: Aries
Celtic Astrology Sign: Alder

Weapon(s) of Choice: Rapier

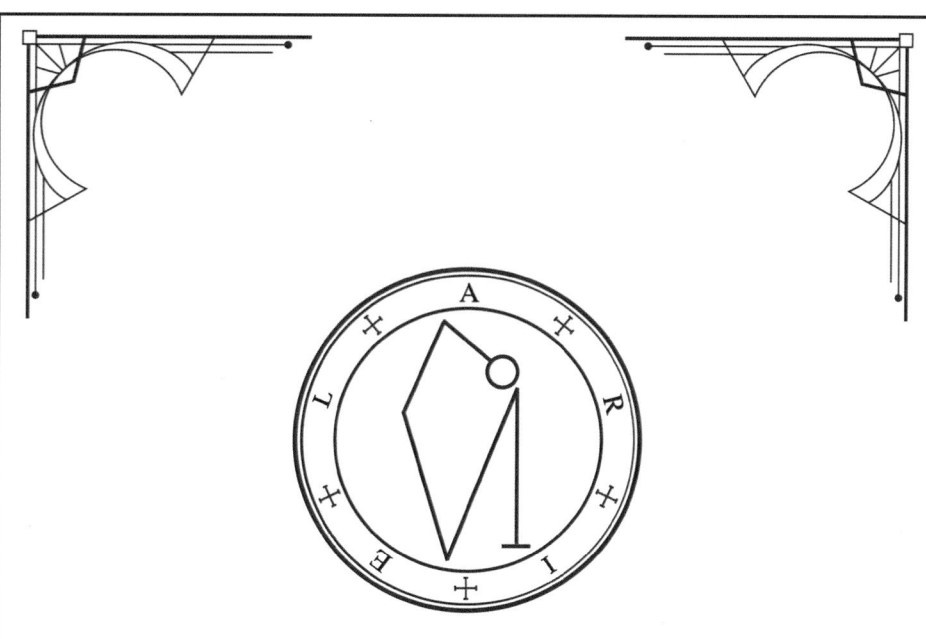

Name Meaning: Lioness of God
Specialties: Courage and Strategy
Circle of Vocation: Angel of Power

Month: March

Color: Maroon

Scent: Peppercorn

Archangel Ariel (AIR-EE-EL), classified as an angel of power, is a fiercely loyal angel and strong warrior. In Heaven, she is responsible for training the other angels to defend themselves. Not all are natural fighters, but it is necessary they know simple maneuvers. She is a general in the Heavenly Army and is a trusted confidante of Archangel Michael.

Ariel oversees strategic planning, and in Heaven, she is responsible for planning watch shifts. Every month, she designates an archangel to manage watch for that month. That angel is then accountable for arranging coverage so that it is a shared effort. This gives Ariel the time she needs to perform other tasks, like tactical training.

Ariel

The Blessed

A Heavenly Compendium

In Druidism, trees are sacred, which is why Celtic tree astrology is a significant part of the culture. Usually, angels are not associated with Celtic tree astrology; however, spiritual guidance is sought through the trees, much like its sought through the angels, which is why there is a correlation. Much like astral astrology, tree astrology has different signs throughout the seasons of the year that each person is born under, and that sign influences one's personality, strengths, and weaknesses.

ᚁ	Birch	The Achiever	December 24 – January 20
ᚂ	Rowan	The Thinker	January 21 – February 17
ᚃ	Ash	The Enchanter	February 18 – March 17
ᚄ	Alder	The Trailblazer	March 18 – April 14
ᚅ	Willow	The Observer	April 15 – May 12
ᚆ	Hawthorn	The Illusionist	May 13 – June 9
ᚇ	Oak	The Stabilizer	June 10 – July 7
ᚈ	Holly	The Ruler	July 8 – August 4
ᚉ	Hazel	The Knower	August 5 – September 1
ᚊ	Vine	The Equalizer	September 2 – September 29
ᚋ	Ivy	The Survivor	September 30 – October 27
ᚌ	Reed	The Inquisitor	October 28 – November 24
ᚍ	Elder	The Seeker	November 25 – December 23

A Heavenly Compendium

Zodiac and Celtic Astrology

Astrology studies the movement of the sun, moon, and planets, and how their positioning influences humans. The zodiac are twelve constellations, or star signs, within the sky that the sun, moon, and planets move through. It is thought that there is a thirteenth zodiac sign known as Ophiuchus, the serpent bearer, that was once a part of the lineup but has been disassociated from traditional astrology. Angels, in general, are associated with the sky, which is why there is an archangel assigned to each sign, even the uncommon thirteenth.

♈	Aries	The Ram	March 21 – April 19
♉	Taurus	The Bull	April 20 – May 20
♊	Gemini	The Twins	May 21 – June 20
♋	Cancer	The Crab	June 21 – July 22
♌	Leo	The Lion	July 23 – August 22
♍	Virgo	The Virgin	August 23 – September 22
♎	Libra	The Scales	September 23 – October 22
♏	Scorpio	The Scorpion	October 23 – November 21
♐	Sagittarius	The Archer	November 22 – December 21
♑	Capricorn	The Goat	December 22 – January 19
♒	Aquarius	The Water Bearer	January 20 – February 18
♓	Pisces	The Fish	February 19 – March 20
⛎	Ophiuchus	The Serpent Bearer	November 29 – December 17

A Heavenly Compendium

Natural Wonders of the World	
Aurora Borealis	Norway
Giant's Causeway	Ireland
The Grand Canyon	United States of America
The Great Barrier Reef	Australia
Harbor of Rio de Janeiro	Brazil
Mount Everest	Nepal
Paricutín	Mexico
Victoria Falls	Zimbabwe

Modern Wonders of the World	
The Acropolis of Athens	Greece
Angkor Wat	Cambodia
The Colosseum	Italy
The Eiffel Tower	France
The Empire State Building	United States of America
The Great Wall of China	China
La Sagrada Familia	Spain
The Taj Mahal	India

A Heavenly Compendium

Wonders of the World

There are three different types of wonders of the world: ancient, natural, and modern. These locations are significant historically, and in the case of the natural wonders, they are a testament to God's handiwork, as these sites display the beauty of Earth. Typically, there are seven wonders within each type, but an eighth is known to exist. Each of the wonders of the world–ancient, natural, and modern–are grouped together and associated with an angel.

Ancient Wonders of the World	
The Colossus of Rhodes	Greece
The Great Pyramid of Giza	Egypt
The Hanging Gardens of Babylon	Iraq
The Lighthouse of Alexandria	Egypt
The Mausoleum of Halicarnassus	Turkey
The Statue of Zeus at Olympia	Greece
Stonehenge	England
The Temple of Artemis at Ephesus	Turkey

Weapons

As warriors, angels of power require a weapon to fight against evil. Each of them is taken to the Forge in Heaven where a weapon is crafted specifically for them. For the archangels, their names are engraved in angelic script on the handle and sometimes decorated with the gemstone linked to them. Other angels throughout the celestial hierarchy have weapons built for them, but doing so is like taking a vow that implies they will answer the call to battle on Judgment Day.

A Heavenly Compendium

Scents

Scent conveys emotion and personality, and each angel carries a unique and pleasant smell that closely relates to their character. Aromatherapy—the practice of using scents, like those of essential oils, for healing—is a way to connect to the angels and has historically been used in spiritual practice.

Frankincense	Spicy and grounding
Jasmine	Strong and musky
Lavender	Delicate and calming
Lily	Rich and floral
Ocean	Airy and refreshing
Patchouli	Intense and earthy
Peppercorn	Warm and spicy
Pine	Fresh and earthy
Rain	Clean and musky
Rose	Light and fresh
Sage	Crisp and cleansing
Sandalwood	Rich and woody
Vanilla	Sweet and comforting
Wood Smoke	Rustic and smoky

A Heavenly Compendium

♃	Jupiter	Tin
♂	Mars	Iron
☿	Mercury	Quicksilver
☽	Moon	Silver
♆	Neptune	Brass
♇	Pluto	Cobalt
♄	Saturn	Lead
☉	Sun	Gold
⛢	Uranus	Platinum
♀	Venus	Copper

Months and Days of the Week

In Heaven, every archangel takes shifts to watch the Earth below, but time in Heaven does not pass as it does on Earth, so the angels educate themselves on the human cycles of the year, like the twelve months and seven days of the week. Certain archangels are assigned to each month and day of the week for watch duties. These assignments have taken on greater meaning, though, becoming the best times to commune with specific angels for guidance.

A Heavenly Compendium

Metals, Planets, and Elements

Physical alchemy is the process of transmuting metals into gold and discovering the elixir of immortality. This elixir is a medicine presumed to give everlasting life and/or cure any disease. The ten metals are the ones used in the actual alchemical process and are connected to the ten planets, while the five elements are the different states of material transformation. The fifth element is often referred to as quintessence, or aether, and is believed to be the most powerful element that unites the other four elements, as it originates from the celestial world.

♁	Quintessence (Aether)		
△	Fire	Water	▽
△ (with line)	Air	Earth	▽ (with line)

Although most of the transmutation process is chemical, there is a philosophical aspect to alchemy that involves spiritual advancement. Spiritual alchemy is where the angels act as guides to assist individuals through a journey of self-discovery to an enlightened state. It mimics the intent of physical alchemy, the soul starting with a basic foundation and transmuting into a higher consciousness.branch, and the tree itself is another way to show how God's energy flows from Heaven through the universe.

A Heavenly Compendium

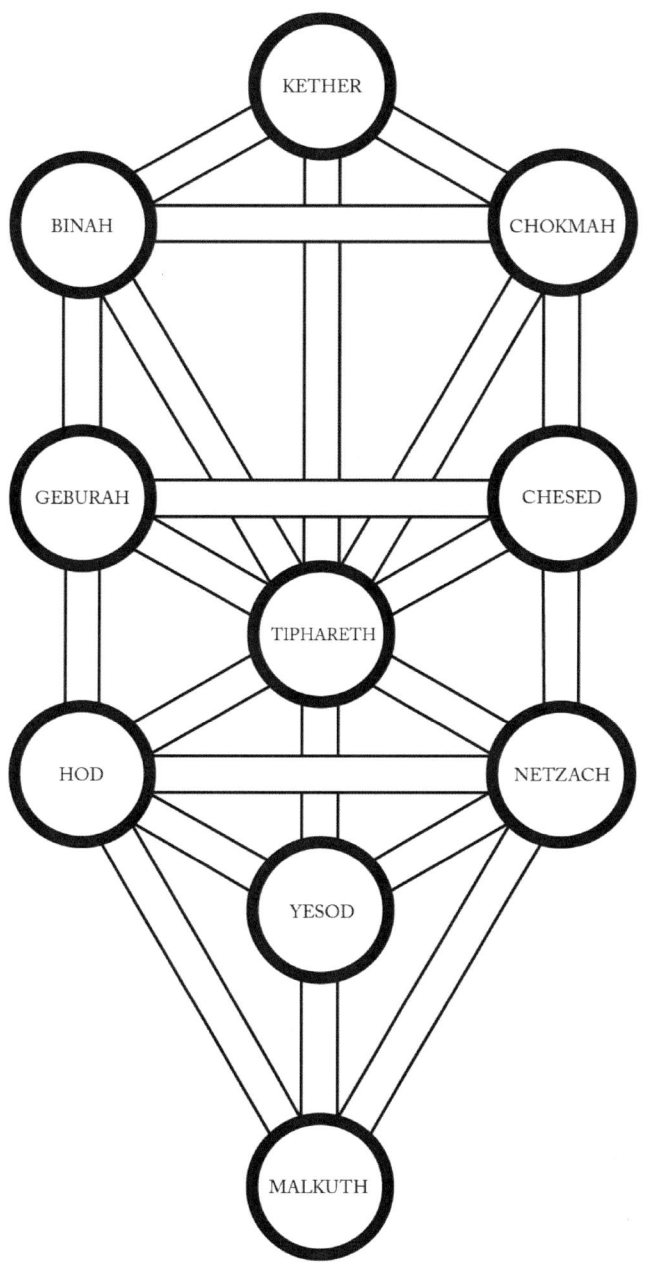

A Heavenly Compendium

Kabbalah

Kabbalah is a Jewish philosophy that seeks to understand the relationship between the divine, material, and astral realms. Those who study Kabbalah and master its teachings are believed to have a deeper connection with God. The Ten Sefirot, shown below, are different attributes or branches of the Kabbalah Tree of Life (source: *The Kabbalah & Magic of Angels*, González-Wippler). An angel oversees each branch, and the tree itself is another way to show how God's energy flows from Heaven through the universe.

Kether	Crown
Chokmah	Wisdom
Binah	Understanding
Chesed	Mercy
Geburah	Judgment
Tiphareth	Beauty
Netzach	Victory
Hod	Splendor
Yesod	Foundation
Malkuth	Kingdom

A Heavenly Compendium

Gemstones

The entire body is made up of energy and affected by it; gemstones are helpful tools to balance energy and to protect from external energetic forces, regardless of whether they are beneficial or harmful. Reiki is a type of therapy that removes energy blockages and distributes energy throughout the body. Gemstones are often used to aid the process. Each gemstone has varying meanings and are chosen for their specific strengths.

Amethyst	Serenity, calmness, wisdom
Bloodstone	Courage, justice, willpower
Citrine	Happiness, good fortune, motivation
Danburite	Harmony, patience, tranquility
Diamond	Purity, strength, faithfulness
Emerald	New beginnings, loyalty, prosperity
Fulgurite	Purification, grounding, manifestation
Iolite	Intuition, self-awareness, stability
Lapis Lazuli	Truth, enlightenment, success
Onyx	Good luck, change, sharpened judgment
Rose Quartz	Love, compassion, emotional healing
Ruby	Power, protection, passion
Tanzanite	Transformation, creativity, communication
Yellow Calcite	Optimism, cleansing of negative energies, inner peace

A Heavenly Compendium

Similarly, auras are invisible colors the body produces depending on energy levels and one's physical and mental well-being. Chakras and auras impact one another, as chakras are smaller energy centers within the larger energy field of one's aura. Every angel has a shade that their aura radiates, and each aura color carries meaning.

Color	Meaning
Black	Darkness, power, mystery, elegance
Blue	Peace, intuition, loyalty, honesty
Gray	Compromise, wisdom, stability, sophistication
Green	Balance, growth, nature, healing
Lavender	Femininity, grace, calmness, purity
Maroon	Strength, courage, sophistication, ambition
Orange	Energy, joy, abundance, positivity
Pink	Emotional stability, harmony, cheerfulness, compassion
Purple	Wisdom, spirituality, creativity, connection to the spiritual realm
Red	High energy, passion, action, leadership
Tan	Stability, reliability, simplicity, warmth
Turquoise	Tranquility, harmony, self-expression, healing
Yellow	Optimism, generosity, happiness, confidence
White	Purity, enlightenment, connection to the divine, rarity

A Heavenly Compendium

Chakras, Auras, and Colors

There are seven chakras, or centers of energy, throughout the human body and each is symbolized by a different color.

 Crown | Purple

 Third Eye | Indigo

 Throat | Blue

 Heart | Green

 Solar Plexus | Yellow

 Sacral | Orange

 Root | Red

A Heavenly Compendium

Similarly, spirit animals—or animal totems—are paired with angels for symbolic significance. Shamanism is the practice of bridging the physical and astral planes, often performed by a person called a shaman. In shamanic rituals, spirit animals act as guides through the spirit realms and aid travelers on their journeys. Oftentimes, these passages are intended for spiritual growth, healing, or affirmation. Each angel is linked to an animal guide and sometimes uses this form to convey messages through dreams or everyday encounters.

Badger	Courage, independence, inquisitiveness
Bear	Strength, protectiveness, agility
Bison	Resourcefulness, fortitude, determination
Deer	Swiftness, grace, gentleness
Elephant	Intelligence, sociability, loyalty
Fox	Intuition, wit, observation
Horse	Vitality, speed, confidence
Jackal	Adaptability, resourcefulness, intelligence
Lamb	Compassion, gentleness, innocence
Lion	Leadership, protectiveness, loyalty
Rabbit	Creativity, adaptability, affection
Ram	Forthrightness, daring, courage
Tiger	Intuition, vitality, strength
Wolf	Sociability, loyalty, leadership

A Heavenly Compendium

Birds and Animals

Birds have a strong association to angels since both are considered messengers. Birds and angels are paired based on the personality traits they share; however, their connection is beyond symbolic. It is physical, too. The angel can call the bird and speak to it or can have them carry paper messages. If needed, the angel can even see through the bird's eyes in the sky.

Bald Eagle	Strength, freedom, courage
Barn Owl	Knowledge, intuition, guidance
Cardinal	Outgoingness, confidence, enthusiasm
Crane	Balance, grace, longevity
Dove	Peace, tranquility, optimism
Falcon	Ambition, independence, observation
Harpy Eagle	Power, wisdom, protection
Hawk	Creativity, fearlessness, precision
Osprey	Abundance, transformation, focus
Peacock	Magnificence, attention, beauty
Puffin	Imagination, sensitivity, affection
Raven	Vigilance, observation, fearlessness
Sparrow	Modesty, resilience, self-reliance
Thunderbird	Power, strength, protection

A Heavenly Compendium

Blessed Angelic Associations

Below are ten topics related to the archangels with brief context as to how these topics correlate to them in general. Not every archangel will be connected to every association, mainly because they are limited in number. Specific connections will be noted in each angel's profile.

Angel of Teaching

    Angels of teaching are angels who possess the capability to teach, otherwise known as Heaven's teachers. They love to learn and absorb new information, so naturally, reading is one of their favorite activities. Many also enjoy writing. Angels of teaching are typically wise and introverted, preferring books to other beings' company.

Angel of Power

Angels of power are angels who possess the capability to fight, otherwise known as Heaven's warriors. They are fierce defenders of Heaven and protectors of Earth. When help is needed, they never hesitate and are eager to assist. Angels of power can detect evil and know how to eradicate it.

Angel of Nature

Angels of nature are angels who possess the capability to protect and care for nature, otherwise known as Heaven's naturalists. They know every plant and animal, and prefer being outdoors at all times. Angels of nature are advocates for the natural world and do not mind speaking up and using their voices for good.

Angel of Music

Angels of music are angels who possess the capability to sing and/or play any musical instrument, otherwise known as Heaven's harmony. Oftentimes, their sounds are calming and inspirational. Angels of music are intuitive, and their main intent is to create music that sparks feeling and emotion.

Angel of the Home

Angels of the home are angels who possess the capability to nurture and/or care for the home, otherwise known as Heaven's caretakers. These angels enjoy cooking, baking, sewing, and tidying up. Organization is key for angels of the home, who are good listeners and always there to offer support.

Angel of Healing

Angels of healing are angels who possess the capability to heal, otherwise known as Heaven's healers. These angels are interested in the science of medicine and practice both holistic and modern approaches. Angels of healing are patient and level-headed, especially in emergency situations.

Angel of Art

Angels of art are angels who possess the capability to create artistic works and/or inventions, otherwise known as Heaven's artists. These angels enjoy painting, ceramics, sculpture, drawing, and metalwork, to name a few mediums. Angels of art are typically curious and friendly with a great interest in the world around us.